"GENEALOGY: A COMPREHENSIVE GUIDE FOR TRACING YOUR FAMILY TREE"

Ink Roots: Ancestry Research

Mollie L. Trammell

Attract Success, LLC

"To my ancestors, whose stories and sacrifices paved the way for my journey. This book is a tribute to your enduring legacy."

CONTENTS

CHAPTER1: INTRODUCTION - THE IMPORTANCE OF FAMILY LEGACY AND GENEALOGY

Welcome to Ink Roots -" Genealogy: A Comprehensive Guide for Tracing Your Family Tree," where we will journey into the world of genealogy and uncover the importance of documenting family legacies.

Embarking on the journey of researching my family's history was an emotional rollercoaster. Each discovery, whether joyous or heart-wrenching, was a part of my past and added a profound layer to my family's roots.

Understanding our origins is key to understanding who we are. My curiosity about my roots led me to explore my family history, a journey that has been both enlightening and rewarding.

As I delved deeper into my family history, I noticed that my ancestors ceased to be mere names and dates. They became more real to me as I learned about their lives, struggles, and triumphs.

Understanding the Value of Documenting Family History

Every family has a story. By documenting our family history, we do not just create a record of the past; we enrich our lives. Our ancestors faced challenges, celebrated success, and navigated life in ways that still show up in our lives today. Documenting these stories preserves their legacy and gives us a deeper understanding of ourselves.

How Family Stories Shape Our Identity

I have found that family stories are like roots—they anchor us, which is one of the main reasons I chose the name "InkRoots." They offer a sense of belonging and continuity, connecting us to something greater than our present existence.

Learning about my great-grandfather's struggles during the Great Depression was not just a piece of history, but a personal connection to the past. His endurance and the legacy he left behind, raising seven sons and later his grandson, my father, inspire me to this day.

Overview of What the Book Will Cover

In this book, you will find a comprehensive guide to building and understanding your family tree. We will start with the basics of genealogy, from gathering records to using online resources. We will explore how to interview family members and provide practical tips, advice, and resources to aid you on your journey. Learn to organize and preserve your findings, ensuring your family's legacy remains for future generations.

Have a detailed record of your family history and how to share it with others. We will also examine the benefits of DNA testing and how it can enhance your understanding of your family's past. It is important to note that DNA testing can reveal unexpected family connections and may uncover sensitive information about health or ancestry.

Therefore, it is crucial to consider the potential emotional and ethical implications before deciding to include DNA testing in your research. Finally, discuss ways to honor and celebrate your family history, from creating a heritage album to planning a reunion.

Why You Should Document Your Family History

As mentioned earlier, documenting our family history is not just about preserving the past—it also has benefits for the present and future. Researching your family history can bring you closer to your ancestors from the past and living relatives. It can also help you better understand yourself by learning about your ancestors' cultures, values, and family traditions.

Recording your family history allows you to create a tangible legacy that flows to future generations. Your descendants will have access to a wealth of information about their roots and heritage, giving them a stronger sense of identity and connection to their past.

Moreover, documenting your family history can also help in medical research and understanding inherited health conditions. Knowing your family's medical history enables you to spot genetic patterns and take preventative measures for future generations.

This book is a comprehensive guide to exploring your family history. Whether you are just beginning or have been researching for years, it offers practical tips, advice, and resources to support your journey.

You will learn about discover methods and tools for researching family history and information about DNA testing. You will also discover how to organize and preserve the information you gather and ways to share your findings with others. Historical records, such as census data and other essential documents, may all provide valuable information about your family's past.

Beyond the technical aspects of documenting your family history, this book also delves into the emotional elements of such a personal and meaningful pursuit. We discuss the importance of storytelling, preserving memories, and ways to honor and celebrate your family's heritage.

Conclusion: This chapter has illuminated the profound impact of documenting our family stories, how they shape our identity, and the invaluable legacy they create for future generations. By uncovering the tales of resilience, triumph, and everyday life from our ancestors, we create a deeper connection to our heritage and a stronger sense of self. It is a bridge that spans time, linking us to the past while guiding us into the future.

CHAPTER 2: HOW TO TRACE YOUR FAMILY TREE

In the first chapter, we explored the exciting world of genealogy and why it matters. If you are anything like me by now, you are ready to uncover the stories hidden within your family tree.

Taking the First Steps

The initial steps of genealogical research might seem impossible, but by following a system and process it can become an enjoyable journey. The key is to start small and build as you go backward through time. I will walk you through my process, sharing tips and short stories from my journey.

Begin with What You Know

The best place to start is with yourself. Print your full name, birth date, and place of birth, such as an identification page. Fill out as complete as possible, any other information or stories is vital to document or list in a folder for future use.

Next your parents and siblings, documenting their details. I also used this process with my InkRoots—Genealogy Packet, which I developed to help organize and track family research. More about that later in the book. For now, start with yourself and work backward.

Next, contact close relatives. Ask them about their memories, collect old family photos, and gather any documents they might have. Birth certificates, wedding photos, and even old letters can hold valuable information.

I remember sitting with my mother and grandmother, sifting through a box of black-and-white images. Each image had a story, and each story added a new branch to our family tree.

Organize Your Findings

Once you have gathered some initial information, it is crucial to organize it; I recommend creating both digital and physical records. Numerous software tools, such as Ancestry.com, MyHeritage, and FamilySearch, are available online.

Many other sites and information are available online. Additionally, for physical copies, consider utilizing the Ink Roots Genealogy Workbook and Ink Roots Genealogy Packet; for more information, see Chapter 12.

For physical records, a simple binder with dividers can work wonders. Divide it into sections for each family branch and organize documents chronologically within each section. This method made it easier to spot gaps in my research.

Setting Goals and Staying Motivated

Genealogy is an intriguing process; strive to enjoy the journey as you discover the past. Establishing clear goals can help keep you remain focused and motivated.

When I began, my initial goal was to learn more about my great grandparents. Achieving that goal felt incredibly rewarding and fueled my desire to uncover more about my heritage and ancestors.

My First Breakthrough

My first significant breakthrough was one of the most thrilling moments in my genealogical journey. After weeks of sorting through documents and online records, I stumbled upon grandchildren from my second cousin on my father's side, resulting in phone and video calls with their family. I also discovered that their father was still living, and I talked with him, my father's first cousin, by videoconferencing.

Resources for Beginners

Knowing where to look for information is essential when you are just starting. Here are resources that I found beneficial:

Local Libraries

Many libraries have genealogy sections with books, local histories, and access to online databases.

Census Records

These can provide valuable information about family members, occupations, and residences.

Church Records

Baptismal, marriage, and burial records often contain key details not found elsewhere.

Online Databases

Websites like Ancestry.com, MyHeritage.com, and FamilySearch.com offer extensive databases and tools to aid your research.

Cemetery Databases

Websites that help you identify grave sites, such as www.findagrave.com, will provide much information for your search.

Conclusion: Starting your genealogical research can seem overwhelming, but it can be a gratifying endeavor with patience and organization. Remember, every piece of information is a step closer to uncovering your family's unique story.

In the next chapter, we will venture further into our research, uncovering family secrets hidden for generations.

CHAPTER 3: UNCOVERING FAMILY SECRETS

I remember making many significant discoveries, including that several of my great-grandfathers were Christian ministers. These revelations helped me understand our family's character, resilience, and faith.

Strategies for Handling Sensitive Information

Of course, not all discoveries are thrilling or desirable. Some secrets buried deep for a reason and discovering them can be like opening Pandora's box. I have encountered stories of infidelity, hidden illnesses, and even criminal activities. Managing this sensitive information requires a delicate touch and much empathy.

In these circumstances, I learned that context is crucial. People make decisions based on their circumstances, often with limited options. Understanding this helped me approach these secrets with compassion rather than judgment. After months of fruitless searching, there was a moment when their circumstances, I learned that context is crucial.

The Rewards of Persistence and Curiosity

Despite the challenges, the rewards of digging into family secrets are immense. I have found long-lost relatives, pieced together stories on the brink of extension and as a result deepened my connection to my roots.

The thrill of having the emotional highs and lows and the ultimate understanding and connection make this journey incredibly worthwhile. Every family secret uncovered, every story pieced together, adds another dimension to our heritage.

Conclusion: Ultimately, uncovering family secrets is more than discovering who did what. It is about understanding where it originated, accepting the good with the bad, and building a fuller picture of our identity. Persistence pays off, not just in the facts we uncover but also in the connections we strengthen and our empathy for those who came before us.

As I continue this never-ending quest, one thing remains clear—family history is not just about the past. It is about understanding and shaping who we are today and who we aspire to become tomorrow.

CHAPTER 4: PRESERVING THE PASTARCHIVING AND DOCUMENTING FAMILYHISTORY

The Importance of Preserving Family History. We have all heard stories about our grandparents or seen old family photos, but how often do we consider preserving those memories for the future?

Family history is more than just a collection of documents, names, and dates. It is our heritage of who we are and where we originated. Preserving this legacy is a gift to our descendants, offering them a window into their heritage and a sense of belonging.

Imagine stumbling upon an old box in your attic filled with letters, photos, and heirlooms, like finding a treasure chest, each item holding a piece of the puzzle that makes up your family's story.

Now, imagine sharing this treasure with your children and grandchildren, letting them experience the joy of discovery just as you did. That is the power of preserving history.

Best Practices for Physical Archiving

Preserving physical documents, photos, and memorabilia requires more than storing them in a box. Here are some best practices to ensure they stand the test of time:

Climate Control

Store items in a cool, dry place away from direct sunlight. Extreme temperatures and humidity can cause damage.

Acid-Free Materials

Use acid-free boxes, folders, and sleeves to prevent yellowing and deterioration.

Proper Handling

Always manage items with clean dry hands to avoid transferring oils and dirt.

Organizing and Labeling

Label each item with relevant information, such as names, dates, and locations. Use a pencil or archival-quality pen to avoid damaging the material.

Categorization

Group items by theme, including tags as family events or distinctive periods. Categorization makes it easier to locate and reference later.

Digital Archiving Techniques

In today's digital age, preserving family history has become easier and more accessible. Digital archiving allows you to create backups, share information with family members, and ensure longevity. Here is how to Begin:

Scanning and Digitizing

Label and only use High-Quality Scans to digitize photos, documents, and other memorabilia. This type of scan ensures that the digital copies are as detailed and precise as the originals.

JPEG for photos and PDF for documents. Future technologies are more likely to support these formats.

Organizing Digital Files-File Naming

Use a consistent naming convention, including crucial preservation details like names, dates, and events. For example," Smith_Jane_Wedding_1985.jp."

Folder Structure

Create a folder on your computer or cloud storage. Organize files by categories such as" "Photo," Letter," and" "Birth Certificate."

Backups-Multiple Copies

Always keep multiple copies of your digital files. Store them on different devices, such as an external hard drive, cloud storage, or a USB drive.

Regular Updates

Regularly update your backups to include new additions and changes. Schedule monthly or quarterly reminders to ensure consistency.

Creating a Systematic Approach

It is essential to do research using a systematic approach to ensure an organized and updated archive. Here is how:

1. **Develop a Routine:** Set aside monthly time to update your family records. This will keep the process manageable and progressing.
2. **Involve the Family:** By involving your family, you can provide relatives with helpful family information, make the process more enjoyable, and encourage other family members to do the same.
3. **Document Sources:** Always note the source of each item, whether it is a photo from an album, or a letter found in Grandpa's attic—credibility and context to your records.
4. **Use Archiving Software:** Use specialized archiving software to manage your digital collection. Programs like Family Tree Maker or Legacy Family Tree offer features designed specifically for genealogical research and archiving.

It is common for families to lose valuable pieces of their history due to poor archiving practices. Preserve and cherish your family's legacy.

Conclusion: Finding information from the past is a thrilling process, and how we preserve this information is paramount to the process.

Properly maintaining a system to safely store your items, whether they are actual photos, stories, or legal documents, is essential.

CHAPTER 5: THE ART OF INTERVIEWINGLEARNING FROM FAMILY ELDERS

Stepping into my uncle's living room, I had felt a mix of anticipation and curiosity. I was so excited to obtain the family stories and to document them before they became lost in time. Armed with a list of questions, a digital recorder, and the hope that he would share the stories that had shaped our family, I was ready to begin.

This chapter is about capturing fleeting moments of oral history that can transform our understanding of who we are and where we come from.

Oral history is the heartbeat of any family tree. The stories, memories, and lived experiences breathe life into the names and dates on your family chart. While documents and photographs provide tangible evidence, personal anecdotes offer depth and color to your family history.

Practical Tips for Conducting Engaging Interviews

Interviewing with a family elder can be both rewarding and challenging.

Here are some practical tips:

Choose a Comfortable Setting

Ensure the environment is free from distractions so everyone feels at ease and more willing to share openly.

Be Prepared

Have your questions ready but be flexible. Sometimes, the best stories come from unexpected tangents.

Use Technology Wisely

A digital recorder or smartphone app can capture every word. Do not rely solely on memory or note-taking; recordings ensure you get all the details.

*Crafting Questions that Evoke Detailed, Personal Stories.

* The key to a meaningful interview lies in the questions you ask.

Here are some strategies to craft compelling questions:

Open-Ended Questions

Instead of asking yes/no questions, use open-ended questions and encourage more information and dialog.

Follow-Up Prompts

If your interviewee mentions a significant event, ask for more details" "How did that make you feel"?" or" "What happened next"?"

Chronological Approach

Sometimes, starting from the beginning of their life and moving forward can naturally unearth stories and memories.

Recording and Compelling Interviews for Posterity

Recording interviews is crucial for preserving these stories for future generations here. Here is how to ensure your recordings are top-notch:

Evaluate Your Equipment

Before starting, ensure your recorder or app works correctly, and that you know how to use it.

Be Mindful of Time

Extended interviews can be tiring for both you and your interviewee. If necessary, break sessions into manageable chunks.

Transcribe the Interviews

Transcriptions make it easier to share and reference the stories later. Many tools are available to assist with this process.

Create a Family Newsletter

Highlight key stories and send them out to family members.

Host a Family Gathering

Share the stories in person at a family reunion or virtual meeting.

Compile a Family Book

Incorporate transcriptions and recordings into family history books that endure for generations.

Conclusion: Interviewing family elders is not just about collecting stories —it is about preserving a legacy. Do not keep the stories to yourself after conducting and recording Family interviews.

Before we move on to the next chapter, I encourage you to contact a family elder this week. Ask them to share their favorite family story, record it, and see how it changes your understanding of your family tree.

The next chapter will explore the fascinating world of tracing your family's migration patterns. These journeys reveal much about the circumstances that shaped our ancestors' own.

CHAPTER 6: MAPPING OUT YOUR FAMILY TREE

Mapping out my family tree was a wonderful experience. It was like embarking on a treasure hunt, each discovery being a gem connecting me deeper to my roots. One of the most helpful tools was utilizing my Ink Roots Genealogy Forms, as by following this format, I could stay consistent and on track.

But the real magic happened when I combined these templates with modern technology. I utilized online ancestry platforms and DNA testing kits to expand my research and draw out a family heritage going back generations. This blend of traditional and contemporary methods transformed what could have been a tedious process into an interactive and engaging adventure.

Utilizing Immigration Records

One of the critical areas I explored was immigration records. These are a goldmine for anyone looking to trace the families' migration patterns. I could track ancestors' journeys from their homelands to their new homes by accessing passenger lists, naturalization documents, and border crossing records. It was fascinating to see the paths they took and imagine the challenges they faced.

Delving into DNA Testing

DNA testing has revolutionized genealogy research. Companies like Ancestry-DNA and 23andMe provide kits that can reveal your ethnic background, connect you with distant relatives, and pinpoint specific regions where ancestors originated.

I remember the moment I received my DNA results. It opened a door to the past, a far more diverse and intricate past than I had imagined. The results showed a mix of European, Jewish, Scottish, Norwegian, and several other ethnicities.

I had no idea of any Jewish heritage until my DNA test. Information enriched my family narrative, and I felt more connected to my roots than ever.

Discovering Ancestral Villages

One thrilling part of my genealogy research was uncovering ancestral villages. Places where my family roots run deep, often spanning centuries.

Online databases and local archives can help you pinpoint these locations, providing a tangible connection to your heritage.

Leveraging Ancestry Technology

Technology has made creating and managing your family tree more accessible than ever. Websites like Ancestry.com and MyHeritage.com offer powerful tools for building your tree, accessing historical records, and connecting with other researchers.

Bringing it All Together

After gathering information, the next step, combine it into a coherent and comprehensive family tree. This involved organizing the data, verifying sources, and filling in gaps.

One of the most helpful strategies was creating a timeline for each family member. This strategy helped me keep track of important dates and provided a broader historical context for their lives. For example, understanding the economic conditions during my great-grandfather's time shed light on his struggles and more about his day-to-day life.

Another helpful tool was the family group sheet, which records vital information about each family unit. By filling out these sheets, I could cross-reference facts and ensure the accuracy of my tree. These forms also made it easier to spot patterns and connections I needed to investigate.

Finally, I compiled all this information into a physical copy and a digital family tree using genealogy software. Utilizing the Roots Packet, I have preserved my family history and research for future generations.

Conclusion: Mapping out your family tree is more than just a research project; it is a journey of self-discovery. By exploring immigration records, leveraging DNA testing, discovering ancestral villages, and using online technology, you can uncover the rich tapestry of your heritage.

*Each piece of information adds a new layer to your family narrative, helping you understand where you come from and who you are.

And remember, you are not alone on this journey. Countless resources, communities, and experts are available to guide you. Uncovering your family history is rewarding and enlightening whether you are just starting or well into your research.

CHAPTER 7: DNA

DNA testing can lead to discovering relatives you never knew existed—like when I uncovered my father's first cousin. Though they were close relatives, they had never met. The thrill of connecting with this newfound relative was genuinely exhilarating.

Updating Your Family Tree

It is crucial to update your family tree as you uncover added information through your DNA results. This dynamic approach ensures that your genealogical research evolves with each discovery, keeping you engaged in your family history.

Ethical Considerations of Genetic Testing

While DNA testing offers incredible opportunities, 'it is essential to consider the moral implications:

Privacy Concerns

Sharing your genetic information with testing companies involves trusting their data security measures. Understand their privacy policies and how they manage or share your data.

Informed Consent

Ensure that all family members who contribute DNA samples are fully informed and give their consent. Unexpected discoveries can impact more than just the individual tested.

Health Implications

Some DNA tests reveal health-related information. Consider whether you want to know about potential genetic predispositions to certain conditions and the emotional impact this knowledge might have.

By navigating these ethical considerations thoughtfully, you can ensure that your exploration of genetic genealogy exploration genealogy is both respectful and responsible.

Conclusion: Incorporating DNA into your genealogical research opens a new dimension of discovery. From understanding your ethnic background to connecting with long-lost relatives, genetic testing can transform your family history.

CHAPTER 8: HISTORICAL RECORDS

Chapter 7 explored how DNA testing can be a powerful ally in genealogy, adding genetic insights to family history research. Let us focus on more traditional methods with Chapter 8, Navigating Historical Records.

For many genealogists, historical records are the backbone of their research, providing critical information throughout their lives. But where do you start? How do you find these records, and more importantly, how do you make sense of them?

This chapter will take you through the maze of historical records, offering tips for effective research, understanding diverse types of documents, and overcoming usual challenges.

Understanding Different Types of Historical Records

Before we dive into the practical details of accessing and interpreting historical records, it is essential to understand the diverse types you might encounter. Each record type can offer different insights into your family history.

Census Records

Census records are a treasure trove for genealogists. Conducted at regular intervals (typically every ten years) they offer a detailed snapshot of a family's living conditions, names, ages, occupations, and places of birth. These documents allow for tracking family movements, household changes and social status through time.

Birth, Marriage, and Death Records

These documents, often vital records, are crucial for building your family tree. Birth certificates can confirm dates and places of birth, while marriage and death certificates can provide additional details, such as a spouse's name and parental information.

Immigration and Naturalization Records

Immigration and naturalization records can be incredibly revealing for families with immigrant ancestors. They often include details about the ancestor's origin, the port of entry, and the date they arrived in their new country. These records can also provide clues about other family members who may have traveled together.

Military Records

If your ancestors served in the military, these records could offer a wealth of information, from enlistment dates and service details to pension records and discharge papers. They can also provide personal insights through letters, photographs, and service medals.

Where to Find and Access These Records

The next step is locating these valuable documents. Fortunately, online, and offline resources are available to help you access historical records.

Online Resources

The internet has revolutionized genealogical research, making finding historical documents much more accessible than ever. Refer to the reference section for information and links to these various online resources.

Ancestry.com: Known for its extensive collection of census records, vital records, and military documents.

FamilySearch.org: A free resource with many records, including birth, marriage, and death certificates.

MyHeritage.com: This subscription-based site provides access to international records, making it ideal for those researching ancestors from different countries.

Offline Resources: Online resources offer incredible convenience, but offline information is invaluable. Local archives, libraries, government offices often house records awaiting digitization. Visiting these places can grant access to original documents and other materials like newspapers, city directories and land records.

Local Archives: Often house records specific to the region, including census data, land deeds, and probate records.

Libraries: Many libraries have dedicated genealogy sections with microfilm collections, books, and access to online databases.

Government Offices: Vital records offices, county courthouses, and town halls often have birth, marriage, and death certificates on file.

Tips for Translating and Interpreting Historical Documents:

Once you have found the records, the next challenge is understanding them. Historical documents can be tricky to interpret due to old handwriting, archaic language, and changes in record-keeping practices over time.

Deciphering Handwriting

Old handwriting can be one of the biggest hurdles in genealogical research. Patience and practice are key here. Start with the basics—compare letters and words you understand to those you do not. Over time, you will get better at recognizing common phrases and names.

Understanding Archaic Language

Language evolves, and terms used in historical documents have different meanings today. Familiarize yourself with standard terms and phrases from your research period. Glossaries and historical dictionaries can be invaluable resources.

Cross-Referencing Information

Always cross-reference information from multiple sources. A single record can contain errors or incomplete data. You can better picture your ancestors' lives by comparing details from various documents.

Overcoming Common Research Challenges

Genealogical research is many times complex. You will encounter roadblocks but keep going. Here are some usual challenges and tips for overcoming them:

Incomplete Records

Sometimes, records are incomplete, in such cases, look for alternative sources. For example, a baptismal record might provide similar information if a birth certificate is unavailable.

Common Surnames

If you are researching a common surname, distinguishing your ancestor from others with the same name can take time and effort. To narrow your search, use additional details like dates, locations, and family relationships.

Language Barriers

If your ancestors came from non-English-speaking countries, you might encounter records in a foreign language. Online translation tools and language-specific genealogical forums can be helpful.

Conclusion: Navigating historical records can be challenging but also enriching. These documents are the keys to unlocking a family's past, providing rich details about your ancestors' lives. Become a more effective and confident genealogist by understanding the distinct types of records, knowing where to find them, and learning how to interpret them.

This chapter has covered the fundamentals of navigating historical records, providing you with the knowledge and tools to make meaningful progress in your genealogical research. In the next chapter, we will explore how to document and share your findings with others, ensuring that your family's history endures for future generations.

CHAPTER 9: FAMILY REUNIONS ANDLEGACY EVENTS

Family reunions are magical gatherings where generations come together. For a fleeting time, we surpass our fast-paced lives and briefly celebrate the roots that bind us. In this chapter, we explore the art and science of planning these reunions, weaving in engaging activities, and turning these gatherings into legacy events that reinforce the ties within our family tree.

Planning and Organizing Family Reunions

Planning a family reunion is not just about setting a date and sending out invitations; it is about creating an experience that will have lasting memories. Every detail matters, from the initial spark of an idea to the final farewells.

Step-by-Step Guide to Planning

Form a Reunion Committee, by forming a resolute committee can help distribute responsibilities. Each member can tackle various aspects, such as location scouting, activity planning, and communication.

Choose a Convenient Location

Ideally, the location should be accessible to most family members. Consider places with sentimental value or central locations.

Budget Wisely

Establish a budget early on, accounting for venue costs, catering, and activities. Encourage family members to contribute to ease the financial burden.

Communicate Effectively

Every detail matters, by utilizing emails, social media, and even handwritten information, we can ensure information sharing. This is highly effective in maintaining accurate information and collecting more documents with a collaborative approach.

Information remains current, accurately reflected, and serves as a wonderful collection of history and family heritage.

Interactive Genealogy Workshops

One of my favorite ways to engage family members is through interactive genealogy workshops. Create stations to share knowledge, scan old photos, or record video interviews.

Storytelling Sessions

Invite the elders to share their stories. These sessions entertain and educate the younger generation about their heritage. My great-uncle narrated tales of ancestors' migration at one reunion, sparking a deeper appreciation for our roots.

Photo Exhibits and Memory Boards

Set up a wall or a table with family photos spanning generations. Include captions with names and dates. This visual representation allows everyone to see how the family has grown and changed.

Using Reunions to Gather and Share Family History:

Reunions offer a unique opportunity to gather and share family history dynamically and engagingly.

Collecting Stories and Artifacts

Encourage attendees to bring family artifacts, old letters, and photographs. Budding historians set up a digitization station to scan and preserve these treasures. You can also create a shared online repository where everyone can upload and access these memories.

Recording Oral Histories: Equip a quiet corner with a camera and microphone, inviting family members to share their recollections. Recordings transform into family documentaries, preserving voices and stories for future generations.

Educational Presentations

If budding historians are in the family, invite them to present their research. These presentations can provide fascinating insights into your family's past, making history come alive.

Fostering Connections

Encourage interaction between different branches of the family. Icebreaker activities and group games can help break down barriers and foster new relationships.

Celebrating Traditions

Incorporate family traditions into the reunion. Whether it is a special meal, a song, or a ritual, these traditions reinforce a sense of identity and continuity.

Creating Lasting Memories

Provide everyone with souvenirs, like a family tree poster, a photo album, or a custom t-shirt. These mementos serve as reminders of the bond shared and the commitment to preserving family heritage.

Personal Anecdote

From my experience, family reunions provide a fantastic opportunity to renew connections, exchange family information, and uncover long-lost stories. A recent death in my family, though a sad occasion, brought us together at the gravesite.

Conclusion: Careful planning, engaging activities, and integrating family history into family events are powerful tools for connecting generations and preserving familial bonds.

These events can deepen your understanding of one's roots and identity. The sense of community fostered at reunions contributes to a legacy and a shared commitment to preserving family heritage.

CHAPTER 10: DIGITAL TOOLS AND PLATFORMS

When I first started exploring my family's history, I relied heavily on physical documents and handwritten notes. However, digital tools have made genealogy more accessible and organized. There are various software options available that cater to diverse needs:

Ancestry is one of the most well-known platforms. It offers extensive databases and intuitive tools for building family trees. I found it particularly helpful for accessing historical records and connecting with distant relatives.

Family Search is a powerful and accessible genealogical resource offering a vast collection of free family trees, records, and resources. Family Search, a trusted resource for those seeking their family history since its 1999 launch, enjoys unwavering support from the Church of Latter-day Saints.

This site allows users to build and explore their family trees, connect with relatives, and access billions of records from around the globe. With its collaborative approach, FamilySearch enables descendants to share information and create a more complete and accurate family tree, all without any cost, empowering everyone to start their genealogical journey.

MyHeritage is an online genealogy platform introduced by an Israeli company in 2003. It offers web, mobile, and software products and services that allow users to build their family trees, upload and browse photos, and search through over 19.9 billion historical records. MyHeritage also provides a genetic testing service which helps users discover their genetic and ethnic background and connect with relatives.

The platform supports forty-two languages and has grown into one of the top-rated ancestry websites in the world through over 19.9 billion historical records.

Geni is known for its collaborative approach. It lets you build a family tree with input from relatives, which can be fun and interactive for the whole family.

Treemily offers stunning visualizations of family trees, which can be particularly appealing to younger generations. The ability to print out these trees as posters is a lovely touch.

Protecting and Data Security

One of my primary concerns when using digital tools was ensuring the privacy and security of my family's data. Here are some steps I took to protect our information:

Choose Trusted Websites

Utilize reputable ones with strong privacy policies and security measures.

Adjust Privacy Settings

Most platforms allow you to control who Can view and edit your family tree and allow you to Adjust these settings to suit your comfort level.

Be Cautious with Sensitive Information

Avoid uploading sensitive personal information, such as social security numbers or detailed financial records.

Regular Backups

To prevent data loss, it is essential to regularly back up your information. Besides maintaining information online, a physical hard copy is necessary in case of loss of digital data and to preserve it for future generations. Most platforms offer automatic backups but securely storing a personal copy is always the best practice.

Family Members Online

One of the most rewarding aspects of using digital tools alone is the ability to collaborate with family members, both near and far. Inviting them to the website offers automatic backups, but securely storing personal copies is always good. I discovered new stories and information that I would not have found alone. Aspects of using digital tools alone are the ability to collaborate with family members and how we made the most of this collaboration:

Invite Contributions

Use the platform's sharing features to invite family members to view and contribute to the family tree.

Hold Virtual Family Reunions

Platforms like Zoom or Google Meet can hold virtual family reunions where everyone shares their discoveries and stories.

Create a Family Newsletter

A periodic newsletter can keep everyone updated on new findings and encourage ongoing participation. Multiple tools are available online, making creating and distributing these newsletters easy.

Conclusion: In this digital age, preserving and sharing our family history has never been more dynamic and interactive. From powerful genealogy software to collaborative portals, today's tools allow us to organize our data efficiently and engage with relatives meaningfully.

Remember, safeguarding our data privacy and security is paramount. By choosing trusted sites and being mindful of the information we share, we can enjoy the full benefits of these digital tools without compromising our privacy.

CHAPTER 11 - PASSING THE TORCH

Passing the torch to the next generation is more than just handing over a collection of documents and photos. It is about igniting a passion for family history that will keep our stories alive for years.

One of the most effective ways to engage younger family members is by sharing intriguing and sometimes surprising stories from our genealogical research.

When I first started exploring my family tree, I had no idea it would lead me to relatives scattered around the globe. The joy of discovering connections through DNA testing and online networks has been remarkable.

For example, finding distant cousins in Scotland and Norway has expanded my understanding of my heritage and piqued the interest of my children and grandchildren.

Methods for Passing on Your Research and Materials: We must meticulously document and preserve our research to ensure our family history survives for future generations. Here are some found particularly compelling:

Create a Digital Archive

Platforms like Google Drive and Create a Digital Archive: Several online platforms offer beautiful keepsakes and offer cloud storage to preserve them for future generations. Additionally, many offer ways to share essential files with family members.

*It is especially important to maintain physical copies of all information as a back up to your online copies. Physical copies are also much more assessable to share with others and easily transferred to one's children.

Compile a Family History Book

Collect stories, photos, and documents into a professionally bound book. Several online services can help you create beautiful keepsakes.

Genealogy Website

One of the many rewarding aspects of my research has led me to create a website, www.genealogybox.com, to share insights and resources on ancestral information. Although the site is developing, it will soon offer packets of pre-filled genealogy forms and other helpful resources to assist others on their research journeys.

Organize Physical Archives

Label and store physical documents and photos in acid-free boxes and folders. By proper labeling and cataloging documents, they are easily accessible.

Host Family Gatherings

Use family reunions or virtual meetings to share exciting discoveries and encourage others to contribute compelling findings.

Inspiring the Next Generation

Inspiring the younger generation to take an interest in genealogy can be challenging, but it is crucial for ensuring our family legacy lives on. Here are a few strategies that I used during my own research:

Make it Fun!

Turn genealogical research into a fun activity. Create a scavenger hunt for family records or organize a storytelling night where everyone shares their favorite family tale.

Use Technology

Leverage social media and genealogy apps to make the process more engaging. Websites such as Ancestry and MyHeritage offer interactive ways to explore family history.

Connect with Relatives

Encourage younger family members to connect with distant relatives and make them part of your process. By doing so, you enable the younger generation to begin to develop an interest in their past heritage.

Highlight Personal Stories

Share the stories that resonate most with you. For example, my children were fascinated to learn about their ancestors who immigrated to America with just a suitcase and a dream. These personal stories make history feel more natural and relatable.

Encourage Participation

Invite younger family members to join their ancestors in your research. Whether helping to organize documents or conducting interviews with older relatives, getting them involved can spark a lifelong interest.

Passing the torch of family history is a responsibility that carries immense privilege and joy. We ensure our family legacy will live on by documenting our research, sharing our stories, and igniting a passion for genealogy in the next generation.

Conclusion: In this chapter, we discussed how vital it is to research your ancestry and utilize various resources to preserve your heritage for future generations.

CHAPTER 12: REFLECTING ON THE JOURNEY AND LOOKING TO THE FUTURE

This concluding chapter summarizes the key lessons learned and a call to action to encourage you to continue this rewarding pursuit.

Understanding Our Roots

By exploring our family history, we better understand who we are and where we come from. It is a way to honor those who came before us and appreciate the struggles and triumphs that shaped our lives.

Documenting family history ensures that the memories of our loved ones survive for future generations. Whether through photos, written stories, or recorded interviews, preserving these memories is a precious gift that keeps giving.

Genealogy is not just about looking back but also about building connections in the present. Sharing your discoveries with family members can create bonds and develop a powerful sense of unity and pride in your heritage.

Inspiring Future Generations

By documenting your family history, you set an example for younger generations. You show them the importance of knowing their roots and encourage them to continue the work you have started.

The impact of documenting your family history extends far beyond personal satisfaction. It contributes to a collective understanding of our societal heritage. Each piece added to the puzzle helps create a fuller picture of our shared past.

When you document your family history, you contribute to a legacy that will outlast you. It is a way to ensure that future generations have a foundation to build their understanding of self and family. It is about creating something enduring—a true testament to the lives and stories that shaped who we are today.

While this book may be ending, your genealogical journey is a continual and rewarding journey. There is always more to uncover, stories to hear, and connections to make.

Here are some ways to continue exploring and preserving your heritage: Join a Genealogy Group and connect with others who share your passion for family history. These groups can provide support, resources, and a sense of community.

Visit Historical Sites

Visit places significant to your family's history. Seeing these locations in person can provide a deeper connection to your ancestors.

Use Online Resources

Websites like Ancestry, MyHeritage.com, and FamilySearch.com offer extensive databases and tools to aid your research. Connect with us on our Facebook Page: My Genealogy Box.

Record Stories

Make it a habit to record the stories of your family members. Whether through written notes, audio recordings, or video interviews, capturing these narratives is invaluable.

Conclusion: Researching and documenting the past is a way to honor our ancestors, better understand ourselves, and inspire future generations.

Coming Soon: "Ink Roots: Genealogy Workbook"

As you continue uncovering your family's history, stay tuned to my upcoming book, "Ink Roots: Genealogy Workbook." This companion guide will provide a collection of forms and templates designed to help you document your family history in detail. From pedigree charts to family group sheets, you will have all the necessary tools to organize and preserve your genealogical research.

Thank you for allowing me to be a part of your genealogical adventure. Remember, the roots of your family tree are deep and robust, and your dedication to preserving this legacy ensures that it will continue to grow and flourish for generations to come.

www.mygenealogybox.com

REFERENCES

Historical Archives

· National Archives and Records Administration. (n.d.). Census records. Retrieved from https://www.archives.gov/research/census. - Smithsonian Institution. (n.d.). Historical manuscripts. Retrieved from https://www.si.edu/research.

Genealogy Websites

· Ancestry.com. (2023). Genealogy data and tools. Retrievedfromhttps://www.ancestry.com.

· FamilySearch. (2023). Family tree building. Retrievedfromhttps://www.familysearch.org.

· MyHeritage. (2023). Global historical records. Retrievedfromhttps://www.myheritage.com.

Critical Topics in "Ink Roots"

Genealogy Research

· National Genealogical Society. (2023). Standards for sound genealogical research. Retrieved from https://www.ngsgenealogy.org.

Ancestral Culture

· Heritage Foundation. (2023). Understanding ancestral cultures and traditions. Retrieved from https://www.heritage.org.

Family History

· Jones, L. (2021). The importance of documenting family stories. *Journal of Family History, forty-six*(2), 123-134. doi:10.1177/0363199021993456

ABOUT THE AUTHOR

Mollie L Trammell

Meet Mollie, a Southern girl with a passion for the past! As the CEO of Attract Success LLC, Mollie has honed her writing and business coaching skills, leveraging a robust academic foundation and firsthand experience to guide aspiring entrepreneurs.

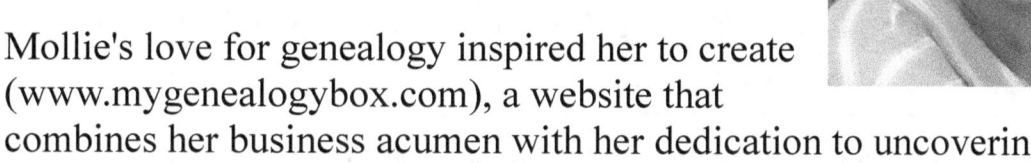

Mollie's love for genealogy inspired her to create (www.mygenealogybox.com), a website that combines her business acumen with her dedication to uncovering ancestral stories. She has also developed a series of genealogy forms, available soon as both a workbook and a packet of forms, to help others on their journey to discover their family history.

BOOKS BY THIS AUTHOR

"Attract Success: System By Design"

Ready to rewrite your life story? Attract Success is here for you! Our system helps transform dreamers into doers by teaching them the tools to unlock a world of positive potential. We believe success is not an endpoint but an ongoing process – and our comprehensive guide shows how each step can lead closer to fulfilling goals.

Clicks To Riches: "Unlocking The Power Of Passive Income: Your Ultimate Guide to Earning Big With Affiliate Marketing"

Introducing Clicks to Riches, "Unlocking the Power of Passive Income:

Your Ultimate Guide to Earning Big with Affiliate Marketing." Authored by Mollie Trammell and published by Attract Success, LLC, this comprehensive eBook is your ticket to unlocking affiliate marketing secrets.

Unplug: "Escaping The Noise For A Focused Life"

Embark on a transformative adventure with "Unplug" - a book that will renew your sense of calm and harmony. Discover powerful strategies like mindfulness and meditation that will relieve stress and nurture your mental well-being.

First Time Author's Guide: "Unlock Your Hidden Writing Potential"

"First Time Author's Guide" is concise and practical yet comprehensive, covering crucial elements like the writing process, self-publishing, and marketing. The eBook demystifies the world of writing and publishing, breaking it into manageable chunks that even the most novice writer can understand.

Daily Focus And Productivity Planner: "Ink And Line"

The Daily Focus and Productivity Planner is more than an organizer—it is a beacon for those dedicated to building excellence. Whether you are tracking habits or setting milestones, it is the perfect companion for your journey.

Planner: "Ink and Line"

"Ink and Line": The Minimalist Weekly Planner for Ultimate Productivity. Unlock efficiency with the "Ink and Line" Planner, where minimalist design meets functional elegance.

Journal: A Compact Guide To Daily Positivity And Growth

Elevate and transform your daily life with our compact and versatile Positive Affirmations Journal. Designed for anyone committed to self-improvement and positivity.